Caleb and Katie's Big Book of Bible Adventures

Alan & Linda Parry

WORD PUBLISHING

Dallas · London · Vancouver · Melbourne

CALEB AND KATIE'S BIG BOOK OF BIBLE ADVENTURES

Copyright © 1993 by Alan and Linda Parry.

Published in the United Kingdom by Hunt & Thorpe
under the title *My First Big Book of Bible Stories*.

Library of Congress Cataloging-in-Publication Data

Parry, Alan 1940–
    Caleb and Katie's Big Book of Bible Adventures / Alan Parry and
Linda Parry
      p.   cm.
    "Word kids!"
    Summary: An illustrated retelling of thirty-six stories from the
Old and New Testaments. Each spread features two children in
modern dress to lead readers into the story.
    ISBN 0-8499-0982-1
    1. Bible stories. English (1. Bible Stories.) I. Parry,
Linda. II. Title.
BS551.2.P375 1993
220.9'505—dc20   92–27866
                                                    CIP
                                                     AC

Printed in Singapore

3 4 5 6 7 8 9 TWP 9 8 7 6 5 4 3 2 1

CONTENTS

THE BEGINNING

"How did the world get here?" asked Caleb.

"God made it," said Katie. "He made it in seven days!"

First He made the sunshine. Then He made the dry land and the seas. He planted trees and flowers on the land and put fish and crabs and octopuses and great big whales into the sea.

Birds and buzzing insects flew in the sky. Then He made the animals. . . .

4

Next God made people. He made a man named Adam and a woman named Eve. He put them in a beautiful garden called Eden.

God said they may eat the fruit from all the trees in the garden—EXCEPT THIS ONE!

Look out! Here comes a long slippery snake! "Hiss," said the snake. "This fruit tastes lovely!"

Oh, dear! Eve ate the fruit and gave some of it to Adam!

Because Adam and Eve disobeyed God, they were sent away from the Garden of Eden. They had to work hard and grow their own food.

NOAH

Caleb and Katie are playing with their toy ark. God told Noah to build an ark, which was like a great big wooden ship.

"Noah," said God. "I am going to send a flood to wash away all th[e] bad things. But because you are good I shall save you and your famil[y] and two each of every animal, bird, and crawling thing."

When the ark was finished, everyone went inside. Then it began t[o] rain. And it rained and rained. And the water rose higher and higher. It rose so high that it covered the tallest mountain. At last the rain stopped, and the ark came to rest o[n] a mountain called Ararat .

After a time Noah opened a window and sent out a dove. It came back with an olive leaf in its beak. So Noah knew that the water had gone down.

When the earth was dry God said: "Open the door, Noah, and let the animals go free."

"Thank you, Lord, for saving us," said Noah.

"Look up at the sky," said God. "See the rainbow! It is my promise that the earth will never, ever be destroyed by another flood."

THE TOWER OF BABEL

At first all the people in the world spoke one language. "Let's build a city," they said, "with a tower that reaches up to the sky! We will become famous." But when God saw it, He said, "I shall mix up their language, then they won't understand one another." And God scattered the people over all the earth, so they stopped building the city.

A NEW HOME

Out of all the people in the world, God chose one man.
"Abraham," said God. "Leave your home in the city and go to the land of Canaan." So Abraham set off. He took his wife, Sarah, and all his sheep and cattle and camels to Canaan.

God blessed Abraham and Sarah in the new land, and they had a baby boy called Isaac. But one day God tested Abraham and said to him, "Give me Isaac as a sacrifice upon the altar!"

Abraham prepared the altar and sadly laid Isaac upon it.

Then, HOORAY! A voice called down from heaven, "Abraham! STOP! Don't hurt Isaac. Now I know that you love me because you are willing to give me your own son!"

When Isaac grew up, he married a beautiful girl named Rebekah. Rebekah gave birth to twin boys called Esau and Jacob.

"Abraham and Sarah lived in a big tent in Canaan."

Esau became a hunter, but Jacob liked to stay home and look after the sheep. One day, Esau and Jacob quarreled. Esau was so mad he wanted to kill Jacob. So Jacob ran away and went to live with his Uncle Laban.

While he was there, Jacob fell in love with Rachel, Laban's daughter.

"Laban, I shall work seven years for you," said Jacob, "if you will let me marry Rachel." Jacob also married Leah, Rachel's sister. And after many more years he took his wives, and their twelve sons, and all their sheep back home to Canaan. Then at last, Jacob and Esau made friends with each other.

9

THE DREAM THAT CAME TRUE

When Jacob's son Joseph was seventeen, Jacob gave him a beautiful colored coat. Joseph's older brothers were jealous. "It's not fair!" they grumbled.

Then Joseph had a strange dream, and he told his brothers about it. "We were all out in the field," he said, "tying up bundles of wheat. Then my bundle stood up straight, and your bundles made a circle around mine and bowed down to it!"

"Huh!" they shouted. "So you think you'll be our king, do you?"

Then one day, when they were far from home, the brothers seized Joseph and threw him into a deep pit. "Ha! Ha!" they laughed. "Now we'll see what will become of your dreams!"

"Help!"

"Look!" cried one of the brothers. "Here come some traders. Let's sell Joseph to them. Then we'll be rid of him forever!"

The traders took Joseph to Egypt and sold him as a slave.

But God helped Joseph. And one night, Pharaoh, King of Egypt, had two strange dreams. Nobody but Joseph could tell what they meant. "There will be seven years with plenty of food," explained Joseph. "And seven years with nothing!"

Pharaoh was so pleased with Joseph, he made him governor of all Egypt. Joseph stored all the extra food through the seven good years. Then, during the bad years, people came to Joseph to buy food. Among them were Joseph's brothers. They bowed low before him.

"Please," they begged, "let us buy some food."

JOSEPH'S DREAM HAD COME TRUE!

"I'm Joseph—your brother!" cried the governor of all Egypt. And then Joseph invited his brothers, and his father Jacob, to come and live with him in Egypt.

SLAVES IN EGYPT

"God changed Jacob's name to Israel," said Katie. "So his family was called the children of Israel."

After many years in Egypt, the children of Israel had grown into a large nation. Now a new pharaoh, who did not remember Joseph, was king of Egypt. "There are too many Israelites in my country," he said. "We must do something about it, or they will take over the whole land!"

So Pharaoh's soldiers made slaves of the people, and treated them cruelly. But still their numbers grew. Finally, Pharaoh commanded: "Throw all the newborn baby boys into the River Nile!"

During this terrible time, Moses was born. His mother hid him for three months. Then she made a little watertight basket for him and placed it in the river.

Pharaoh's daughter came down to the river to bathe. She found the little basket among the reeds. And when she saw baby Moses, she loved him so much, she took him home to the palace and brought him up as her own son.

"Let God's people go!"

72

When Moses was grown up, God said to him: "I have seen how cruelly the Egyptians are treating my people. Now, go to Pharaoh and tell him to let my people go!"

But Pharaoh refused to listen to Moses. So God sent ten terrible plagues against the Egyptians.

First the rivers turned to blood. Ughhh!

Then frogs and gnats and flies swarmed over everyone. Oooh!

And millions of locusts ate up everything in sight. And there were five more plagues even worse.

Then at last, after the tenth plague, Pharaoh cried out, "Let the people go!"

"Let the people go!"

MOSES AND THE GREAT ESCAPE

Moses led the children of Israel out of Egypt toward the Red Sea.

But LOOK OUT! Here comes Pharaoh's army!

"What shall we do?" cried the people. "We're trapped!"

"Watch this!" said Moses. And he held his hand out over the sea.

"Whoosh!" A strong wind blew. And God made a path through the sea.

"Yippee!" shouted the people. "Now we can escape." And they went across the sea on dry ground.

"After them!" yelled the soldiers, as Pharaoh's army charged along the sea path behind the children of Israel.

When the Israelites were safe on the other side, Moses held his hand out over the sea again.

"Splash!" The water came together again, and the cruel Egyptian soldiers drowned in the sea.

JOSHUA THE CONQUEROR

When the Israelites eventually reached Canaan, Joshua became the new leader.

"God will drive out the people of the land," said Joshua, "so that we may live here in peace."

But the people in the great walled city of Jericho kept their gates locked and barred.

Then God thought up a plan to take Jericho. . . .

Joshua and his soldiers marched around the city once a day for six days. Seven priests, each carrying a trumpet, went in front.

On the seventh day, Joshua and his soldiers marched around seven times. Then all at once, the priests blew their trumpets, "Truuump!" And the men gave a mighty shout, "Yaaah!"

Suddenly there was a mighty CRASH, and the walls of the city fell down flat!

GIDEON TO THE RESCUE

When the children of Israel had lived in Canaan for some years, the Midianite army invaded the land. Hundreds and thousands of Midianite troops were camped in the valley, ready to attack.

The people cried to God for help, and God chose Gideon to rescue them.

That night, Gideon took just three hundred men and surrounded the camp. Each man carried a trumpet, and a jar with a torch inside.

The men waited quietly in the darkness. Then all of a sudden, they gave a great BLAST on their trumpets and SMASHED their jars on the ground. And holding their flaming torches high, they shouted, "For the Lord and for Gideon!"

And all the Midianite soldiers ran away!

SAMSON THE STRONG

"Samson was so strong, he killed a lion with his bare hands!" said Katie.

"And he killed a thousand Philistines with the jawbone of a donkey!" said Caleb.

Now the Philistines had invaded the land, and God had given Samson great strength to overthrow them. Samson had been dedicated to God from the time he was a baby and had vowed never to have his hair cut.

But one day, Delilah, Samson's girlfriend, persuaded him to tell her the secret of his strength. Then, while he slept, she had his hair cut! Samson's strength had gone!

The Philistines captured Samson and put out his eyes. Then they held a great feast to celebrate, and they brought Samson out of prison to make fun of him.

But Samson took hold of the two pillars that held up the building and prayed: "Please God, give me my strength just once more!"

And he pushed at the pillars with all his might—"CRASH!" The huge building came tumbling down, killing all the Philistines.

17

THE GIANT WARRIOR

"Come on! Come and fight me—if you dare!" yelled Goliath to the Israelite army. "If one of you can kill me," he roared, "then we Philistines shall be your slaves!"

The Israelites were terrified. For Goliath was over nine feet tall!

But David the shepherd boy, said, "Don't be afraid. I will fight Goliath." Then David ran toward the Philistine. He put a stone in his shepherd's sling and slung it. "SMACK!"

The stone hit Goliath on the forehead. And the giant fell down dead!

"Look how tall Goliath is!"

THE SONGWRITER

David played the harp and wrote many songs that we call psalms. Caleb and Katie like the Twenty-third Psalm best.

The Lord looks after me like a shepherd,
He gives me everything I need.
He takes great care of me.
Even if troubles come my way,
I won't be afraid, Lord,
Because you are always near me,
And will come to my rescue.
You give me every good thing.
I have more than enough.
Your love and kindness
Will be with me all through my life,
And in the end you will give me
Life, forever more.

David became the greatest king of all Israel. And God promised that one day, His own Son would be born into David's family.

THE RICHEST MAN IN THE WORLD

"Ask for anything you want," God said to King Solomon, "and it's yours!"

"Give me wisdom," said Solomon, "so that I can rule your people well."

God was pleased with Solomon's reply. "Because you have asked for this," God said, "you will not only become the wisest, but also the richest and the most famous man in all the world!"

King Solomon built a beautiful temple in Jerusalem. All the cups and bowls were made of solid gold. Solomon made a navy of ships and traded gold, silver, apes, and monkeys. He had twelve thousand cavalry horses and fourteen hundred chariots.

The Queen of Sheba traveled many miles to hear Solomon's wisdom.

When the people saw it, they fell to the ground and cried, "The Lord is God! The Lord is God!"

At the end of Elijah's time on earth, God used a whirlwind to take him to heaven in a chariot of fire.

A RIDE IN A FISH

"Jonah was also one of God's prophets," said Katie.

"Yes, but God sent him to Israel's enemies, the Assyrians," said Caleb.

"Jonah," said God. "Go to Nineveh and tell the people there to stop their wicked ways."

But Jonah did not want to go to Nineveh. Instead, he got on a ship and sailed far away.

So God sent a great storm on the sea, and the ship began to sink.

"Throw the cargo overboard," yelled the sailors, as they tried desperately to row for shore.

"The storm is all my fault," groaned Jonah. "I'm running away from God." When the sailors heard this, they were terrified.

"Throw me into the sea," said Jonah, "and the storm will stop."

So the sailors threw Jonah overboard! Immediately the storm stopped. But Jonah sank down and down to the bottom of the sea.

"Help!" he cried, as a great fish swallowed him up. "Please God," prayed Jonah—all sea-weedy inside the fish—"Save me!"

Then the fish opened wide its enormous mouth and spat Jonah up onto the beach.

"Go to Nineveh," said God again. And this time Jonah went. The people of Nineveh believed Jonah's message. They stopped being bad, and prayed to God instead.

25

CAPTIVES

"Israel would not pray to God or follow His ways," said Katie. "They worshiped Baal and were bad all the time."

"Because you will not serve me," said God, "you shall serve strangers in a foreign land."

And so the King of Assyria invaded the land, captured many of the people and took them away.

Then God sent the prophet Jeremiah to warn the people in Jerusalem. "Stop being wicked," he begged. "Or you too will be taken captive."

For forty years Jeremiah cried out in the streets of Jerusalem. But the people hated Jeremiah and made fun of his warnings.

They beat him and put him in prison. And once he was put into a deep, dark, muddy well.

Jeremiah wrote the warnings down in a book, but the king tore it up and burned it in the fire.

"God will send you away to another land," said Jeremiah. "But after seventy years, He will bring you home again."

And that's what happened. Nebuchadnezzar, King of Babylon, came with his army. He captured all the people and burned down the city of Jerusalem.

"Turn to God and He will save you!"

THE LIONS' DEN

"Daniel was among the captives taken to Babylon," said Caleb.

Daniel loved God and prayed to him every day. And because he was wise and clever, the king made him governor of all Babylon. This made the Babylonian governors jealous. "Why should an Israelite slave be over us?" they complained. "We must find a way to get rid of Daniel."

So the governors thought up a sneaky plan. . . .

"Your Majesty!" they said as they bowed low to the king. "Your governors have agreed that you should give orders that no one is to pray to any god or man, except you, for the next thirty days. Anyone who disobeys," they continued, "SHALL BE THROWN TO THE LIONS!"

The king agreed, and the wicked governors crept round to Daniel's house and found him praying to God as usual. Then the governors raced back to the king. "Daniel has broken your law," they cried. "We found him praying to his God!"

When the king heard this, he was very upset, and tried to find a way to rescue Daniel. But the law could not be changed, so Daniel was thrown into the lions' den.

"Help!" cried Daniel as he fell onto a great, growling lion.

"Grrr!" roared the lion.

The next day, the king ran to the lions' den. "Daniel, oh Daniel!" he called out. "Has your God been able to save you from the lions?"

"Oh King," cried Daniel. "God has sent His angel to shut the mouths of the lions. I'm not hurt at all!"

"Hooray!" shouted the king. "Hooray for Daniel! Hooray for God!"

The king set Daniel free and arrested the wicked governors.

Then he sent a letter to all the people in his empire:

"I command that everyone, everywhere, pray to the God of Daniel. For God saved Daniel from the lions!"

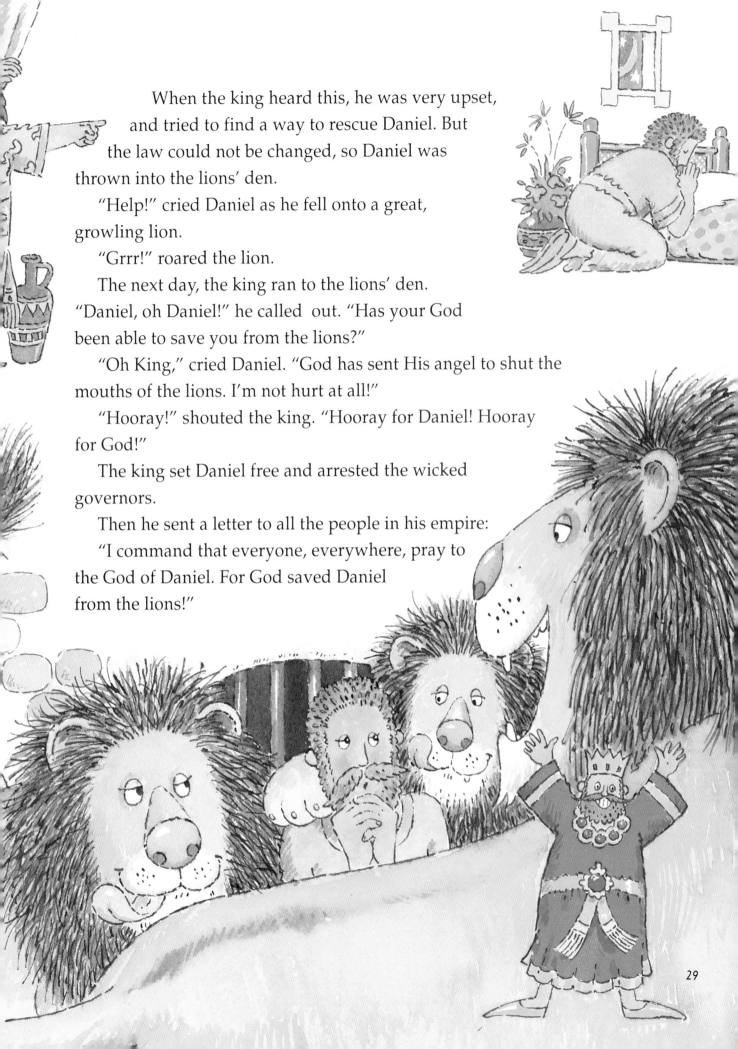

QUEEN ESTHER

"Esther was a captive, too," said Katie. "She was so beautiful, the king asked her to marry him!"

One day, the king chose a man named Haman to be Prime Minister. Everyone had to bow down to Haman because he was so important. But Mordecai, Esther's cousin, refused to do so because he knew it was against God's law.

Haman was furious. He made plans to kill Mordecai and all of God's people throughout the empire.

When Mordecai learned of Haman's evil plot, he sat in the street outside the palace, "Ayeee! Ayeee!" he wailed. And he threw dust on himself to show how upset he was.

Esther's servant ran out with some clean clothes for Mordecai. "What's the matter?" he asked.

Mordecai explained what had happened,

and when Esther heard of it, she pleaded with the king. "Wicked Haman plans to kill all my people," she wept.

"What?" yelled the king. And he ordered his guards to arrest Haman. Then the king made Mordecai Prime Minister instead.

And Mordecai told all his people to celebrate at a certain time every year because Queen Esther had saved them from their enemy.

GOD'S PROMISE

After seventy years of captivity, the children of Israel finally learned to follow God's ways and put away their pagan idols.

Then, Cyrus, the new king, issued this command:

"I, Cyrus, ruler of the whole world, decree that a temple should be built in Jerusalem for the Lord God of heaven. All His people who are in exile may now return to Jerusalem to build the temple to the Lord their God."

So at last, God's promise came true, and the people left Babylon and returned to Jerusalem. King Cyrus gave them back the golden bowls that Nebuchadnezzar had taken from the temple may years before. And the people of Babylon gave them presents, and provided donkeys and food for their journey.

Then, after they were settled in their new homes, work began on the temple. When the foundations were laid, the priests BLEW their trumpets and CRASHED their cymbals, and everyone shouted:

"Hooray! The LORD is GOOD!"

"Hooray! His LOVE is FOREVER!"

"Hooray!"

THE BABY IN THE MANGER

"Later when Rome ruled the world," said Caleb, "there were Roman soldiers all over the land of Israel."

"I decree that a census be taken of all the people throughout my empire!" proclaimed Caesar Augustus, the Roman emperor.

Everyone had to return to their family's hometown and register.

In the little town of Nazareth, in Galilee, Joseph the carpenter and his young wife, Mary, were preparing to set off for Bethlehem in Judea, King David's birthplace. Both Mary and Joseph were descendants of the king.

A few months earlier, before she was married, Mary had a very strange visitor.

"Hello, Mary," said the visitor. "I'm the angel Gabriel. I have brought you a message from God!"

"What—what is it?" stammered Mary.

"You have been chosen to be the mother of God's Son!" announced the angel. "You must name the baby, Jesus."

When Mary and Joseph reached Bethlehem, the inn was full of travelers.

"My baby's coming!" cried Mary. "What shall we do?"

"There's room in the stable," said Joseph. "I'll get it ready for you."

When Jesus was born, Mary wrapped Him in linen clothes and laid Him in a manger.

Then God sent His angel to tell the good news to some shepherds who were out in the fields with their sheep.

"Christ the Lord, the Savior of all the world, is born today!" cried the angel.

The shepherds left their sheep and ran to Bethlehem. There they found Mary and Joseph and saw the baby Jesus lying in the manger, just as the angel had told them.

A STAR IN THE EAST

"The Romans had made Herod king of Judea,"
said Caleb. "He lived in a palace in Jerusalem."

Far away in the East, some wise men were studying the stars.

"Look!" shouted one. "There's a bright new star in the sky!"

"It's the sign that the new King of Israel is born!" cried another.
"Let's go to Jerusalem to see him.

When they reached Jerusalem, they went to the palace and asked
King Herod, "Where is the newborn king? We have come to worship
him."

Herod was troubled. "Newborn king?" he cried. "I'm the only king
around here!"

Sadly, the wise men left the palace. Then all of a sudden—
they saw the star again!

"HOORAY!" they cried. The star went before them and
led them to where the baby Jesus was in Bethlehem. The wise
men knelt down before Him and gave Him presents of gold,
frankincense, and myrrh.

After they had gone back to their own country, King
Herod sent soldiers to Bethlehem. "Kill all the newborn baby
boys!" he ordered. "Then we'll be rid of this new king!"

But God sent His angel to warn Joseph. "Quick!" the angel cried. "Herod is searching for the child. Get out of Bethlehem and escape to Egypt."

Mary and Joseph and baby Jesus stayed in Egypt until the death of Herod. Then they returned to their home in Nazareth.

A TRIP TO JERUSALEM

When Jesus was twelve years old, He traveled to Jerusalem with Mary and Joseph to keep the Passover Festival.

After the celebrations, they started off for home. But Jesus stayed behind in Jerusalem. Mary and Joseph didn't miss Him at first. They thought He was with His friends among the other travelers. But later when He didn't show up, they got worried and started searching for Him.

They searched among their friends and relatives. They searched among the baggage and in the tents. They searched along the trail.

But still they could not find Him. So they went back to Jerusalem and searched there.

Then, at last, after three days they found Him—in the temple!

"Jesus!" cried Mary. "We've been looking for you everywhere!"

"Why did you need to look?" asked Jesus. "Didn't you know I'd be here, in my Father's House?"

Jesus was sitting among the teachers, listening to them, and asking questions. All who heard Him were amazed at His knowledge and understanding.

Then He returned to Nazareth with Mary and Joseph. And Jesus grew up tall and strong, and He was loved by everyone around Him.

A VOICE FROM HEAVEN

"John the Baptist was Jesus' cousin," said Katie.

God chose John before he was born to be the one who would prepare the people for Jesus.

John lived in the desert and wore rough clothes made of camel's hair. He ate locusts and wild honey.

Crowds of people went out into the desert to hear John teach. "Turn to God and be baptized," he cried. "Then God will forgive your wrong doings."

One day, while John was baptizing people in the Jordan River, Jesus came to him. "I want to be baptized, too," he said.

"You, Lord?" said John. "But you have done no wrong. Surely it is I who should be baptized by you!" But Jesus insisted, and John lowered Him into the river.

LOOK! As Jesus came up out of the water, the Spirit of God came down from the sky like a dove and rested on Him.

LISTEN! "This is my own dear Son," cried a voice from heaven. "I am very, very pleased with Him!"

"Let's go!" they cried. And they leaped out of the boat
and followed Jesus.

Jesus chose twelve disciples. They traveled all over Galilee teaching
the people about God and healing their sick.

"Love one another," Jesus taught. "And you
shall be called the children of God."

43

THE PICNIC BASKET

Large crowds gathered around Jesus to hear Him teach. It had been a long day, and the sun was sinking low in the sky.

"This is a lonely place, and the people are hungry," the disciples told Jesus. "Send the people away, so they can buy themselves some food to eat."

"You give them something to eat," said Jesus.

"But it would cost a fortune to feed all these people!" cried Philip.

"How much food have we got?" asked Jesus.

"This boy has five loaves of bread and two fish," said Andrew. "But what's the use of that? There are thousands of people here!"

"Make the people sit down," said Jesus. Then He thanked God for the bread and the fish, and gave a piece of each to all the people.

And what do you think? There was enough food for everybody! Everyone ate till they were full!

And afterwards the disciples collected twelve basketfuls of leftovers!

WALKING ON WATER

After the crowds had gone, Jesus went up into the hills to pray. But the disciples set off in their boat for Gennesaret on the other side of the lake.

When night fell, Jesus looked out across the lake. The disciples were in trouble! A strong wind was blowing, and their boat was tossing about on the waves. Jesus came to them— walking on the water!

"Ayeee!" they shrieked. "It's a ghost!"

"Don't be silly!" called Jesus. "It's me!"

"If it's really You," shouted Peter, "let me come and meet You."

"Come on then," Jesus shouted back. So Peter scrambled out of the boat and started walking on the water toward Jesus. But when he saw the rough waves all around him, he began to panic.

"Help!" he cried out. "I'm sinking!"

"Give me your hand," cried Jesus. "Just believe: and you'll be safe!"

Then suddenly, as they climbed back into the boat, the wind stopped and the lake became still.

"You really *are* the Son of God!" exclaimed the disciples.

When they landed at Gennesaret, crowds of people brought their sick to Jesus. And all who touched even the edge of His coat were healed.

47

JESUS RIDES ON A DONKEY

Jesus was on His way to Jerusalem. Crowds of people were following Him. Bartimaeus, a blind man, sat on the roadside, begging.

"What's all that noise?" he asked the people.

"Jesus is passing by," they told him.

So Bartimaeus called out to Jesus, "Jesus! Help me! Help me!" he shouted.

"Be quiet!" yelled the people.

But Bartimaeus shouted even louder, "Jesus! Son of David! Help me!"

When Jesus heard Bartimaeus, He stopped, and said to him, "What do you want me to do for you?"

"Oh, teacher," said Bartimaeus, "I want to see!"

"All right," said Jesus. "Then see!"

And all at once, Bartimaeus *could* see! He jumped up and followed Jesus.

Along the way a man named Zacchaeus was waiting for Jesus. But he was too small to see above the crowd. So he climbed a sycamore tree.

When Jesus came to the tree, He looked up and said, "Zacchaeus, come down! I want to go to your house today!"

"Hooray!" shouted Zacchaeus as he scrambled down the tree. "Jesus is coming to *my* house!"

When they reached Jerusalem, Jesus rode into the city on a donkey.

Crowds of people came to meet Him. They spread out their coats on the road and laid palm leaves before Him.

"Hooray! Here comes the Savior!" they shouted.

"God bless the King of Israel!"

SUPPER TOGETHER

Every day, Jesus taught the people of Jerusalem in the temple.
"Don't copy what your religious teachers do," warned Jesus. "For they
only want the praise of men. But you must learn to please God."

This made the teachers furious. "Who does Jesus think He is?" they
cried. "The people should listen to *us*, not to the son of a carpenter!"

Then the chief priests and teachers met together and made plans to
put Jesus to death.

It was Passover time, and Jesus and His disciples were having
supper together. But one of the disciples, Judas Iscariot, loved money
more than Jesus. He crept out of the house, into the dark night, and
went straight to the chief priests.

"What'll you give me if I tell you where Jesus is?" he asked them.
And they gave him thirty silver coins.

After supper, Jesus went out into a garden to pray, "Father, help me to do your will," He prayed.

Suddenly, Judas arrived with an angry mob armed with swords and clubs. They arrested Jesus and took Him to Caiaphas, the High Priest.

The disciples were terrified. They all left Jesus and ran away.

THE CROWN OF THORNS

The religious leaders were gathered at Caiaphas's house. They were looking for witnesses who would lie about Jesus, so they could sentence Him to death. But the witnesses could not agree amongst themselves, so at last Caiaphas asked Jesus, "Are you the Son of God?"

"Yes," said Jesus, "I am."

"Blasphemy!" shouted the High Priest. "We don't need any more witnesses! What is your verdict?"

"Death!" they shouted. "Death!"

In the morning they sent Jesus in chains to Pilate, the Roman Governor. They accused Jesus of many things. But Pilate could find no wrong in Him. So Pilate took a bowl of water and washed his hands in front of all the people.

"I am not to blame for the death of this just man," he said.

Then Jesus was whipped and a crown of thorns placed on his head. After that he was led away to a place called Golgotha—The Place of the Skull. There Jesus was hung on a cross and crucified. At twelve noon it suddenly became as dark as night. Then, at three o'clock, Jesus died. And all at once, the sun shone again, and a great earthquake shook the ground! The rocks split open and many good people rose out of their graves and walked the streets of Jerusalem. And the great curtain in the temple was torn in two from top to bottom. By giving His life, Jesus had removed the barrier between God and the people!

ALIVE AGAIN

Two of Jesus' friends, Joseph and Nicodemus, took the body of Jesus down from the cross and wrapped it in strips of linen cloth. They laid it in a new, unused tomb that had been cut out of a wall of rock. Then they rolled a huge stone across the entrance.

Three days later, a woman named Mary Magdalene came to the tomb with some spices to anoint Jesus' body. But she found the great stone rolled aside and Jesus' body gone!

She ran back to tell the disciples. "The tomb is empty!" she cried.

Peter and John ran to the tomb and went inside. They found the linen cloths that had been wrapped around Jesus' body. "What—what's happened?" they wailed. Then sadly they went back home.

But Mary stood outside the tomb, crying. Then suddenly, she saw two angels dressed in white sitting inside the tomb!

"Woman, why are you crying?" they asked.

"Because they have taken away my Lord," she sobbed. "And I don't know where they have put Him."

Then she turned around, and someone was standing behind her.

"Mary," He said.

"Jesus!" she cried. "YOU'RE ALIVE AGAIN!"

POWER FROM HEAVEN

"After Jesus was alive again, He also appeared to His disciples," Caleb told Katie.

One day, while they were talking together on the Mount of Olives, Jesus said to His disciples, "Do not leave Jerusalem until you have received the gift of the Holy Spirit."

Then Jesus rose up to the sky and disappeared into the clouds. And all at once, two angels stood among them. "Jesus has gone to His Father in heaven," they said. "But one day, just as He went, He will return!"

On the day of Pentecost, the disciples and all Jesus' friends were gathered together in Jerusalem.

Suddenly, there came the sound of a great roaring wind, "Whooosh!

Whooosh!" The noise of it filled the house where they were meeting. Then flames of fire appeared and touched each person in the house. And they were all filled with the Holy Spirit.

Everyone began talking in foreign languages.

Many people from different lands were staying in Jerusalem that day. When they heard all the noise they ran to the house. And when they got there, they were all surprised because each one heard the disciples teaching about Jesus in his own language.

"Turn to God, believe in Jesus, and be baptized," cried the disciples, "and you shall receive the gift of the Holy Spirit."

A BLINDING LIGHT
FROM THE SKY

Now many people in Jerusalem began to believe in Jesus. But a young man named Paul, who was also called Saul, hated the believers. He went from house to house and dragged them off to jail. Then he set off for Damascus to arrest the believers there. But just before he reached the city, a blinding light from the sky shone down upon him.

"Ow!" wailed Paul, as he fell to the ground. Then he heard a voice calling him:

"Paul, Paul, why are you persecuting me?"

"Who are you?" Paul cried out.

"I am Jesus!" said the voice.

"Where—where are you?" Paul cried. He stood up, but he couldn't see! He was blind!

His friends led him by the hand into Damascus.

Then, in a dream, God spoke to a man named Ananias.

"Go to Paul and pray for him," He said.

"But Lord," said Ananias, "that man hates your people."

"Go," said God. "For I have chosen Paul to be my servant."

So Ananias went to Paul and prayed for him. And all at once, Paul could see again!

SHIPWRECKED

"It's true," cried Paul. "Jesus is alive!"

Soon Paul went out telling everyone the good news.

He traveled all over the Roman Empire teaching people about Jesus. But many people disagreed with Paul. And one day, while he was in Jerusalem, a mob nearly beat him to death. He was arrested by Roman soldiers and bound in chains.

Since Paul was a Roman citizen, he refused to be tried in Jerusalem. He knew his enemies planned to kill him there.

"I appeal to Caesar!" he said.

"All right," said the Roman Governor. "You have appealed to Caesar, and to Caesar you shall go!"

So Paul, along with some other prisoners, was put on a ship bound for Italy.

But a strong wind blew up on the sea and forced the ship off course.

"Lower the topsail," ordered a sailor.

"Throw out the cargo," cried another.

The terrible storm raged on and on.

Then at last, one of the sailors shouted, "Land ahoy!" And they raised the sail and headed for shore.

But the ship hit a sandbank, and the violent waves began to break it apart.

"Jesus is alive!"

"Abandon ship!" shouted the captain.
Everybody jumped overboard and swam safely ashore.
When Paul eventually reached Rome, he taught the
people there about Jesus—just as he did wherever
he went.

THE VISION

Paul wrote many letters to the believers who were scattered throughout the Roman Empire. Some of the disciples wrote about Jesus' life. These letters and accounts became part of our Bible.

Churches were set up where believers could gather together to worship God. Always, though, the chief priests and the Roman rulers tried to stamp out their beliefs.

When the disciple John was an old man, he was sent away by the Roman emperor to the tiny Island of Patmos. While John was there, he saw a vision from God. John wrote the vision down in a book and sent it to the churches. Today it is the part of the Bible called Revelation.

In the vision John saw a new heaven and a new earth. Everything that was bad and ugly had gone. Only peace and beauty remained.

Then John heard a loud voice saying:

"Now God Himself will live with His people, and He will be their God. He will wipe away all tears from their eyes, and there will be no more death or crying or pain. All that has gone forever. LOOK! I am making all things new!"